My Cat is Ignoring Me!

50 Ways to a Happy Healthy Pet

My Cat is Ignoring Me!

50 Ways to a Happy Healthy Pet

Peter Wedderburn

Illustrated by Per José Karlén

spruce

An Hachette UK Company
First published in Great Britain in 2009 by Spruce
a division of Octopus Publishing Group Ltd
2–4 Heron Quays, London E14 4JP.
www.octopusbooks.co.uk
www.octopusbooksusa.com

Distributed in the U.S. and Canada for Octopus Books USA
Hachette Book Group USA
237 Park Avenue
New York NY 10017.

ISBN 13 978-1-84601-340-9
ISBN 10 1-84601-340-2

A CIP catalogue record for this book is available from the British Library.

Printed and bound in China
10 9 8 7 6 5 4 3 2 1

CONTENTS

Caviar? Oysters? What food can I give her to make her love me?

Junk food or haute cuisine? Should I read the cat food label?

Crunchy or juicy? Dry food or tins and sachets?

I think she's too fat. How can I break this to her gently?

How can I keep her teeth clean without making her hate me?

HISSY FITS 40

I know a dog is a 'lesser' being, but could they like each other?

I know she's in a mood, but why does she have to pee on my sofa?

She ignores me all the time. How can I get her attention?

She gets all cuddly, then suddenly bites me!
What is she thinking?

She wants to sit on the table. How can I teach her not to (nicely)?

She hates car journeys. How can I cheer her up on trips?

She drags live prey through the cat flap. Help!

What's wrong with the scratching post I bought her?

She's being bullied by the next-door tomcat. What can I do?

She's in a mood because I'm going on holiday.
What shall I do with her?

FELINE FUN 56

She keeps bringing her friends around. How can I keep them out?

She looks bored. How can I make her home more interesting?

How about giving her a gentle massage? Any tips?

Would the sweet scent of aromatherapy oils help her to relax?

How can I make a pedicure more fun for her?

She doesn't like her toy mouse. Any ideas for better play objects?

How can I help her to have a long life, as well as a happy one?

Would she be happier if she had her own family?

LOOKING AFTER HER NINE LIVES

How can I make my cat let me groom her?

She hates the vet. Do I need to take her there?

How do I choose a good cat vet?

The vet costs a fortune. Any cheap options?

Why should I give her a worm dose?

I think it hurts when she eats. Could she have toothache?

She isn't itching, but could fleas be making her miserable?

She hates injections. Does she really need those vaccines?

I want her to be fit. What can I do?

She doesn't want to wear her collar. Does she have to?

Give her tablets? You must be joking!

Introduction

Cats are very different to human-loving, owner-pleasing dogs. Cats are independent creatures who seem only ever to do their own thing. In feline current jargon, cats don't even have owners: they have 'guardians' with whom they choose to share a home.

Cats can come across as unappreciative of their human consorts, and many people wonder what they could do to make their cats reciprocate with a little more affection and attention. Are there any 'tricks of the trade' that could help to make an aloof, arrogant feline into a cuddly, affectionate cat?

If your cat is already a people-loving puss, you may still wonder if you are catering properly to her needs. How can you be sure that you are allowing her to live the healthiest and happiest way of life? There are numerous information sources dedicated to cat care, but cat owners often have simple questions that remain unanswered. This book aims to resolve some of those queries, with practical, uncomplicated advice.

This volume contains 50 ways to ensure you are giving your cat the best possible lifestyle, and includes tips on how to make your cat a little more appreciative of her human companions. Keeping a cat is an enjoyable and rewarding experience, or should be. After reading this book, you will be able to improve the cat–human relationship in your home, so that it IS more fun – for both of you.

CHAPTER 1
pick of the litter

How do I choose a happy healthy cat?

Simple: choose a happy healthy cat in the first place. As tear-jerking as a snivelly animal with runny eyes and waxy ears is, health problems, such as cat flu viral infections, can be lifelong issues, which is why it's crucial that your cat's engine purrs from the word go. Deny every instinct that tells you that the hissing, snarling kitten in the corner can be tamed: it can't.

Most humans end up like our parents and so do cats. It's a genetic thing, so it's worth meeting the parents for a dosage of home truths. Tomcats, however, tend to be the worst form of absentee fathers, so don't hold too much hope in meeting dad. Plus, the old Jesuit saying, 'Show me the kitten [boy] at seven weeks old and I will show you the cat [man]', rings true. A calm, relaxed kitten is most likely to turn into a friendly, easy-going adult cat.

Of course, there are exceptions – the sofa-shredding kitten that transforms into a purring lap-cat and the half-wild kitten that becomes a calm, contented adult – and sometimes your heartstrings will tug to the extent that you choose an animal regardless of its health and nature. But as a rule of thumb, go for the cute, healthy-looking cat that will warm your heart and your sofa for years to come.

13

Boy or girl?
Does it make any difference?

What is sex when it comes to sparkling personality? Seeing as most cats are neutered before maturity anyway, you'll be choosing on the assets of their character, rather than their gender. Both male and female cats can be wonderful companions, and both sexes also can be cantankerous bullies. If you already have a cat, avoid the all-girls-school social stresses by having a mix of sexes to break up the tension.

Also, it's a little cheaper to have male cats neutered than females, but the saving is pennies in your pocket. The difference will buy you a couple of big bags of cat food, not a yacht.

Long hair or short?

If only we humans could master tongue grooming, hair appointments would be a thing of the past. Self-grooming is enough for shorthaired cats to maintain shiny, tangle-free coats without the need for a frenzy of shampoos and hairbrushes. Longhaired cats, however, especially pure-breeds like Persians, will need your help in the more difficult-to-lick places such as behind the ears and under the tail. If you want the exotic beauty of a longhaired cat, be prepared to make good friends with the brush and comb, or grit your teeth and bear paying a vet or groomer to clip off matted fur.

Fur balls, a common cause of vomiting in the cat world, are less common in shorthaired cats, so let your yukkiness tolerance influence your decision. Finally, how house-proud are you? Hairier cat – hairier carpet. A simple equation.

What about a rescue cat?

Claim your good-citizen badge by choosing the homeless moggy, but go carefully! Albert Einstein said, 'Men marry women with the hope they will never change. Women marry men with the hope they will change. Invariably they are both disappointed.' Cats are more like men than women: don't assume their personalities will change dramatically.

Cats can live for twenty years or more, so anticipate having to share your life with this creature for a big chunk of it. Avoid the skittish, bad-tempered variety that will take your hand off when you demand a space in your own bed.

What sort of cat carrier is the best?

Cats lounge: they'll airport lounge, cocktail lounge and 'your' lounge. But journeys involve little to no lounging and invariably lead to either the vet or the cattery – at the prospect of an injection you'd be equally difficult to stuff into a box. That said, you can make travel less stressful by choosing a cat-friendly carrier. It needs to be big enough so she can stand up and turn around; should be designed so she can see out without feeling completely exposed to the world (put a blanket over the carrier if there are wide open gaps); and ensure the door catches are solid and there is no way she can escape. There are wire cages, plastic carriers and fabric hold-all types, and you can go fancy, glitzy or plain. Chances are, although you've gone to all this trouble, she's having none of it.

17

How should I welcome her into her new home?

Time to put in your cat eyes. Have you got high-up resting places (from which your cat's sense of superiority can be satisfied), hiding places (cats like to have their own secret moments), scratching posts (nail filing is not a luxury in the cat world), a cosy bed (electric heating pads are a MUST for the 21st-century moggie), and a few interesting toys? Also, install a plug-in Feliway diffuser, which fills the air with soothing pheromones, so that when your cat walks in, she'll have an immediate sense of coming home. Pheromones are the feline equivalent of wafts of freshly baked bread or freshly ground coffee.

18

Home alone?
Or is happiness a crowd of cats?

Toes attacked at breakfast by an attention-seeking kitten? Then try getting her a small, furry, feline playmate. Many cats end up as best buddies, but the wrong mix of personalities can be a less than fun experience. It only takes a few cats streaking past you in terror or fury, and some smelly damp patches of urine on curtains and carpets, for you to long for the days of solo puss. My own rule of thumb is 'no more than three', unless your budget can stretch to frequent visits to the dry cleaner and sessions with the cat psychologist.

CHAPTER 2
kitty litter and cat naps

Indoors or outdoors?
Where will she be happiest?

Car accidents? Predators? Is your cat's safety keeping you awake at night? Indoor cats may be safer, but outdoor cats can prowl about to their heart's content, which they LOVE to do. Make a compromise. In the daylight she may go outside, with the proviso that the personalized cat flap will let her in if she gets cold, wet or tired. But at night, the time when most car accidents and cat fights occur, the cat flap will not open. Your house, your rules.

Should I give my cat her own key so that she can let herself in at night?

There will be no shimmying up or down the drainpipes and no jumping in and out of windows. With a microchip cat flap, such as a Petporte cat flap, you control her comings and goings. For those of you with a large feline family or cat-loving disposition, it can be set to accept up to twelve different microchip numbers and you can set a curfew. The cat flap automatically detects light levels, so you can make sure that your cats are safely kept inside during the hours of darkness. See www.petporte.com for more information.

Her place or mine?
Where should she sleep?

A cat will, no matter the obstacles in her path, always find the most comfy, coziest bed. It's a sixth sense.

Another place they LOVE is high-up places where they can lazily survey the room by simply lifting their heads, and her preference is your duvet. You, however, may not enjoy her snoring and snuffling or being woken by a sudden weight on your chest as she repositions herself for extra warmth.

Create an alternative. In a high-up spot, place a deep-pile, sheepskin-type fleece blanket with a plug-in electric heat pad beneath it. Plug in a Feliway diffuser beside it and suddenly your own bed won't seem quite so appealing to a cat.

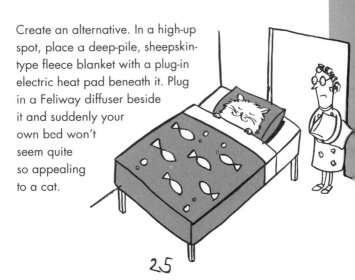

Choosing her bathroom suite: what type of litter tray is best?

The three most important aspects of litter trays are size, depth and roof. If you get these wrong, your cat may decide to choose a bathroom location elsewhere in your home.

The more space she has the less likely it is she will go elsewhere, so choose as big a tray as you can fit comfortably into her bathroom area. Be practical when it comes to the depth, too. Spillage is definitely unwanted, but a kitten or arthritic granny-cat can't always clamber over the high sides easily; and just because you panic whenever you've forgotten to lock the bathroom door doesn't mean your cat craves privacy also. Covered litter trays can cause claustrophobia, so remove the cat-flap door, so she feels less shut-in.

What type of litter material will she prefer?

Cat litter: used by cats, chosen by humans. You may prefer the de-odourized, easy-clean, flushable version, but if she doesn't like it your carpet and your nerves will be the ones to suffer. More important than choosing something exotic is clean litter material, so change it often. Start off with the type that your kitten or cat is already used to, then make any changes gradually. That funny stain on the bathmat will be a tell-tale sign of her reaction to your purchase.

She left a 'number two' in my (now ex-) boyfriend's shoe. Why?

You feel stressed by it? Imagine how stressed she must have been to embark upon such an extreme endeavour. It may have been a one-off, but if it happens repeatedly, there must be something making her feel ill-at-ease in her normal bathroom area. Try some new litter trays and new litter materials, but if it continues, professional advice is definitely called for. Boyfriends may not always be replaceable.

CHAPTER 3

fat cats and
picky pets

What type of food bowl will she prefer?

Plastic is far from fantastic. Ceramic or stainless steel bowls don't become scratched and grimy over time and prevent possible allergic skin reactions. Dinner-excited cats tend to push their plates around, so to stop food spillages choose a bowl with a rim, rather than a flat plate. Also, if you're feeding dry food, don't leave a small mountain of food piled in a bowl. Hide small amounts of kibble around the house instead, so that your cat has to hunt for them. Cats enjoy the challenge and the tasty reward; plus it keeps their brain cells energized.

Why does she insist on drinking from the toilet?

Here comes the science: fresh water from the tap contains chlorine, which dissipates when water is left standing. This means your cat finds toilet water delicious. However, the inevitable moment when she falls in should motivate you to discourage her choosing this source of hydration. Keep the toilet lid closed and try giving her filtered, boiled (and cooled) or bottled water in her bowl. She won't like water by her food bowl, so have a few small bowls dotted about the house. Better again, get a cat fountain, which supplies trickling, filtered water continually. She'll be charmed.

Caviar? Oysters? What food can I give her to make her love me?

Money can't buy you love, but it can buy very expensive, good-quality cat food. She'd wear diamonds if she could, so you know not to scrimp on a cheap alternative – cheaper foods equal cheaper ingredients. Apply the maxim 'you are what you eat'. Cats on a top-quality diet ooze good health, so give her a month or two for the premium diet to kick in.

Junk food or haute cuisine?
Should I read the cat food label?

Decoding the jargon on the ingredients label can be a tricky task. 'Meat and animal derivatives' can describe any meat or animal by-product, without specifying what it is or even which species it comes from. This allows manufacturers to hide the not-so-impressive ingredients, and it enables them to change the protein source with every batch without having to change the label. There are over 4,000 permitted chemical additives that can be used in pet food without individually naming them, and plenty of these additives are know to cause hyperactivity in children. Imagine what they are doing to poor puss! Whenever you can, choose more natural foods with as few artificial additives as possible.

Crunchy or juicy?
Dry food or tins and sachets?

Shake up the boring world of cat food with a combination of the moist and dry. Moist food (tins and sachets) tends to be enjoyed more than dry food by cats, and is more like a 'natural' cat diet with high levels of protein and moisture and low levels of carbohydrate. But dry foods are very convenient, less smelly, less likely to go off and they can help to keep a cat's teeth healthy. Try a small moist meal once or twice daily, supplemented with some dry food. At different times in your cat's life, for different reasons, you may want to give more or less of either moist or dry food, but it's best if she is familiar with both.

I think she's too fat.
How can I break this to her gently?

She hift the responsibility. Get the vet to weigh her at her annual check up, and he can break the news. As you console her afterwards, tell her that about one in four cats is overweight, so she's not alone. The vet will offer her some simple ways to fight the flab. The usual rules of fewer calories, more exercise can be made to sound more palatable if you talk about 'tasty, light food and more play'. It's important that she stays around her ideal weight, because as in humans, obesity is linked with health complications that you could both do without, including arthritis, heart disease and diabetes.

How can I keep her teeth clean without making her hate me?

Just like you, your cat's fangs need regular brushing. However, the odds of her allowing you to stick a strange plastic, bristly object into her mouth on even one occasion, never mind after every meal, are not good. If a kitten has been trained into tooth brushing from an early age, then it may be a possibility, but for most cats, you'll need hypnosis or total sedation. Alternatively, try the next best thing: special prescription-only dry diets, available from vets, that simulate natural abrasive chewing.

CHAPTER 4
hissy fits

I know a dog is a 'lesser' being, but could they like each other?

Cat and dog might be mortal enemies, but there are a few tricks to bring out the white flag. Starting with a chilled-out cat and a calm, obedient dog can be key to a happy menagerie, and catching them while one, but ideally both, is young is also a great start to the peacekeeping process.

The wide-eyed innocence of puppies and kittens makes them difficult for any creature to dislike strongly, so place one of the two in a large wire mesh cage at the start, preventing either from lashing out until they've grown accustomed to one another. Prolonged time in each other's company may be enough to forge a truce, but, as with humans, it's impossible to force a friendship.

I know she's in a mood, but why does she have to pee on my sofa?

Feline shrinks have named this phenomenon 'inappropriate elimination'. There are many causes, but stress of some kind is often involved. Whether there is a new cat bully living nearby, your new girlfriend in her sofa space, or a new type of litter in her tray, something is rubbing her fur up the wrong way. Clean up the piddled area properly and visit your vet sooner rather than later before a one-off accident becomes a life-long habit.

CLEANING UP PIDDLED PATCHES

1. Clean up with a warm, mild solution of biological washing powder.
2. Rinse with warm water.
3. Apply a spray of surgical spirit (do a patch test first to make sure that the surface will not be damaged).
4. Dab the surface dry.
5. Spray on Feliway, a bottled pheromone that will make your cat less keen to go back to the same place, as it will smell so pleasant to her.

She ignores me all the time. How can I get her attention?

Cats are proud creatures, so be prepared to indulge her. She's far too smart to be won over by you playing hard to get, so swallow your pride and do some good, old-fashioned sucking up. Get a new toy and play games with her; get down on your knees to have a chat while she eats her dinner; and when she is sleeping, sit beside her and pet her. Just as long as no one sees you making a fool of yourself, it will work out well.

She gets all cuddly, then suddenly bites me!

Swishing tail? Ears pinned back? Looks like Dr Jekyll, yes? Wrong. She's Mr Hyde. She's peeved and about to sink her teeth into your forearm. Be careful with body language. Some cats aren't into smothering, and would much prefer you to play with them than give them cuddles. Short periods of petting are best, and if she tenses up, move away. She'll curl up on your lap when she's ready. If it's not working out, she needs to see a shrink.

What is she thinking?

Look into her eyes and ask her. She will look back at you with her sphinx-like gaze and the mystery will remain. It is part of the charm of cats – the inscrutability. Do they know something we don't know? Is there some hidden depth? Is something going on beyond the knowledge of simple humans, on a different level altogether? Or is she just wondering what's for supper and which bed will be the most warm and comfy?

She wants to sit on the table. How can I teach her not to (nicely)?

You sit at the table, so why shouldn't she? It has a fabulous vista, often accompanied by a selection of delicious snacks, reading materials and a warm computer keyboard.

Be crafty. Make the table less fun. Cut out a large piece of card and stick double-sided tape to it in a grid-like pattern, leaving the sticky side up. When you go out, leave the card on the table. If she does climb onto the table, she will find it a distinctly unpleasant experience.

She hates car journeys. How can I cheer her up on trips?

She's caterwauling, the kids are shrieking 'Are we there yet?' and you've only just left home. She'll never be into life's journeys, but you can make them a little comfier for her. Choose as big a cat carrier as you can, so that she has plenty of space, and include a litter tray if possible. Make sure she won't be hungry, and travel at night, if possible, as she is more likely to sleep. Give her some familiar bedding and perhaps an old sweatshirt of your own to snuggle into. Spray some Feliway pheromones into her cage before you leave, then top them up every few hours to give her an ongoing sense of comfort.

She drags live prey through the cat flap. Help!

Cute, fluffy cat? Or mean, blood-thirsty predator? She brings her prey home with her because it is a safe place to finish them off and eat them at her leisure. She won't judge you in any way for whatever you do with the prey. Do as you wish: rescue the poor wee creature if you can; finish it off if it is badly injured or just shut the door and leave them to it. Nature is tough, and cats are part of it.

What's wrong with the scratching post I bought her?

There's a trail of shredded fabric leading from your couch back to a peacefully purring pussycat. Do you wring her neck or realize that her scratching post does not live up to the desirability of the sofa when it comes to using her nails? Try finding her a similar surface to the sofa or some corrugated cardboard to cover the scratching post, and make sure the post is tall enough for her to scratch at full stretch. Perhaps even dangle some toys off it and sprinkle catnip around the base to make it more attractive than the sofa.

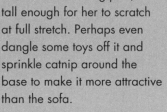

She's being bullied by the next-door tomcat. What can I do?

Run Forest run! Scaredy cats can't be trained into superheroes, so aiding her swift getaway is your smartest option. Give her sneaky escape routes, such as a microchipped cat flap, so she can rush inside unpursued. Plan some stepped ledges around the garden to make it more difficult for him to corner her and give her plenty of toys indoors so that she won't get bored inside. If he continues to be beastly, negotiate to 'time share' the two cats. Agree set days to keep each of your cats indoors, so that she can enjoy time outside in the knowledge that Top Cat is temporarily locked up.

54

She's in a mood because I'm going on holiday. What shall I do with her?

Boarding cattery or house sitter? Some catteries are genuinely five-star establishments, with piped music, heated beds and pheromone-infused air conditioning. If you can book her into a place like this, she will enjoy her holiday as much as you enjoy yours. But do your research. There are also plenty of poor-quality catteries that are best avoided. Many cats prefer to stay at home where they can spread out luxuriously in their new-found independence, over every bed, sofa and floor, with a house sitter either in residence or visiting regularly. This works especially well if there's three or more animals, and it can also be cheaper.

CHAPTER 5
feline fun

She keeps bringing her friends around. How can I keep them out?

There's a mob of cats inhabiting your living room and what can you do? Chances are they're poor company and have antisocial bathroom habits. Time to employ a bouncer in the form of an automated, magnetic cat flap (see page 24) that only your cat's collar can open. Or go for the cat flaps that will only admit cats implanted with nominated microchip numbers. You can set it up to allow her to bring her well-behaved friends home, while excluding those from less salubrious backgrounds.

She looks bored. How can I make her home more interesting?

Take a walk on the wild side. Does your home give her the chance to indulge the wild animal inside her? Are there high surfaces to jump onto and obstacle-course style activities? Can she gaze out of the window with an air of superiority? Visit the Feline Advisory Bureau website at www.fabcats.org for lots more tips on making a cat-friendly home.

How about giving her a gentle massage? Any tips?

Do you enjoy stroking, kneading and 'passive touch'? So does puss. That's why we so instinctively stroke cats. There are multiple books available on pet massage therapy, but trial and error is probably the best way of finding out what suits your own feline friend. Gently squeezing the ear tip between a finger and thumb is very soothing for some cats, but others find it intensely irritating. Many cats are expert masseurs themselves – lying on their owners, kneading their paws up and down.

Would the sweet scent of aromatherapy oils help her to relax?

Danger! A cat's metabolism works very differently to yours and she lacks some enzymes needed for processing common compounds present in some herbs and plants. Remember, too, that her sense of smell is much more sensitive than yours, so a scent that is pleasant to you may be overpowering to her. The safest type of 'aromatherapy' would be to use pheromones – natural, odourless (to humans) chemicals that make animals feel comforted. You can buy cat pheromones, called Feliway, as a spray and as a plug-in vapourizer for a room. You won't notice a pleasant smell (or any smell at all), but your cat will feel happily de-stressed.

How can I make a pedicure more fun for her?

I'm sure your pedicures don't involve having the ends of your toes squeezed with a sharp metal tool, and if they do, perhaps you should consider changing beautician. Nail clipping can be stressful for cats, so it's important to get them used to being held firmly from kittenhood onwards. Gently squeeze their feet, as if you are shaking their paws, as part of this firm handling. Only when your cat is used to this type of close physical contact should you attempt nail clipping. Remember, she can sense your hesitance and will fight tooth and nail to get away. If in doubt, ask your local vet nurse to do it.

She doesn't like her toy mouse. Any ideas for better play objects?

Mouse, schmouse. Who cares? Certainly not your cat. She's vastly more intelligent than you think, so you'll need to get creative. Fur. Feathers. Leather. Grass. Choose materials that stimulate her natural prey – dangly, stringy toys laced with catnip are much more exciting. Let her chase the bright point from a laser pointer, just don't frustrate her as she can never catch it. To prevent this, place that boring toy mouse under a chair or settee and end the game by directing the pointer at it. She can then grab the mouse and take it away with her, with a sense that she has 'won'.

How can I help her to have a long life, as well as a happy one?

There's no feline elixir of life. Cats can live into their twenties, but there's no guarantee. Feed her the best diet that you can afford and, as she ages, give her more moist food to ensure she has a high level of water consumption, which is better for her kidneys. Also, create for her a stress-free, cat-friendly environment. Focus on her from time to time, noticing subtleties like how much water she drinks and how fast she breathes. Take her to the vet at least once a year for a physical check-over and perhaps for urine and blood tests. Remember that one human year is seven cat years, so things can change quite rapidly for her compared to a human.

Would she be happier if she had her own family?

If you have heard cats procreating in the garden, you will realize that it does not sound like much fun. The process of kittening is not as enjoyable as chasing a laser pointer light across the carpet. And a horde of young kittens hanging off your mammary glands is much harder work than snoozing alone in a pool of warm sunshine. I am quite sure that if she could, your cat would thank you for having her spayed at the recommended age of around four months.

CHAPTER 6

looking after
her nine lives

How can I make my cat let me groom her?

It is her body, not yours, so cooperation is vital for what can end up as a losing battle. Get cats used to grooming from kittenhood. A once-weekly comb and brush is a simple routine that takes only a few minutes, and it performs a double function of getting your cat used to regular contact with a brush, while removing small knots and mats before they take on a Rastafarian dreadlock style. Leave it too late and the matted fur may be too dense to remove with a comb, and your cat may refuse to allow you anywhere near her with a grooming implement anyway. If this happens, you then need to revert to Plan V – a visit to the vet for the removal of matted fur with electric clippers under sedation. Such drastic action should be enough to convert her to regular grooming.

She hates the vet.
Do I need to take her there?

A healthy cat is a happy cat. Ideally, her visits to the vet should be kept to a minimum, but she does need her once-yearly check-up. Cats can be clever at hiding problems that need treatment such as sore teeth and irregular heartbeats. Your vet will weigh her, give a thorough physical once-over, administer any necessary vaccinations and parasite control, and listen to your tales of her idiosyncrasies. The annual bundling of the cat into the clinic should be enough to prevent further visits during the year, even if her sharp-clawed resistance might suggest that it's more hassle than it's worth.

How do I choose a good cat vet?

The best way to choose a cat vet is by word of mouth, but you should do a trial visit (without cat) to have a look for yourself. Does the clinic look presentable? Is there handy car parking, so you don't have far to carry your stressed-out cat? Is the waiting room 'cat only', or at least is there some way of keeping noisy dogs out of the way of anxious cats? Are the reception staff friendly people who genuinely like cats? How long are the appointments? And when you eventually take your cat, if she strongly dislikes the vet, choose another vet, even within the same practice, and if she dislikes all vets, at least choose one that YOU like.

DR
o

The vet costs a fortune. Any cheap options?

Simple answer: no! Cheap options result in consequences like amputation instead of fixing a broken leg, or euthanasia instead of an appointment with a pet counsellor. A much better answer is to budget for high-quality vet care from the start by taking out a pet insurance policy from kittenhood onwards. If you are genuinely hard-up and cannot afford insurance, the animal charities, such as the PDSA and the Blue Cross, do offer good-quality vet care at an affordable price on a means-tested basis.

Why should I give her a worm dose?

Hold your stomach…kittens get roundworms from their mother's milk and older cats get worms of various types from hunting prey and from nibbling fleas that they find in their coat. For the sake of both human and cat health, regular worm doses need to be given. Every three months is the average for adult cats, but this does depends on factors like the area where you live, how much hunting she does and her contact with other animals. Remember, spot-on wormers mean you no longer have to struggle to ram a golf-ball sized tablet down her throat.

I think it hurts when she eats. Could she have toothache?

Cats tend to suffer from the type of toothache that hurts when the tooth is touched, rather than constant throbbing pain. So if you think it hurts her to eat, you could be right. Take her to the vet, who will be able to tell from looking at her teeth (and possibly using a delicately placed probe). Dentists have tried using fillings to fix holes caused by decay in cat teeth, but they tend to fall out. The best answer is simple extraction of painful, diseased teeth. A tooth can't hurt the cat when it's in the waste bin, and the tooth socket soon heals over to become part of a very functional, comfortable and healthy mouth.

She isn't itching, but could fleas be making her miserable?

Even the cleanest, most pampered cat can pick up fleas, whether by being close to other cats or just by walking past a place where another cat has been sitting. Fleas make some cats itch furiously, but other, non-allergic, cats can be crawling with fleas without a single scratch. A once-monthly, anti-flea drop from your vet is the safest way to prevent any flea-related issues. Just don't insult her by telling her why you are squeezing that vial between her shoulder blades. Like humans, cats sometimes have the mistaken perception that only street moggies get fleas.

She hates injections.
Does she really need those vaccines?

Even the scientists are out on this one. In recent years evidence has suggested that some modern cat vaccines may last for three years or more, but the product licences are still based on immunity studies of only one year's duration. Most vets still suggest once-yearly vaccines, to be on the safe side. The frequency of vaccination for any cat should be approached on an individual basis, considering genuine risks and needs. Talk to your vet, but make sure your cat isn't listening – she'll always settle for the 'no-vaccine' option.

I want her to be fit. What can I do?

If your cat isn't into becoming Miss Universe, you might have to make her gym experience more appealing. Cat gyms are well-designed toy combinations, with multiple ledges for cats to clamber onto, swinging toys for them to chase, and surfaces (both vertical and horizontal) for them to scratch. Try sprinkling catnip all over it, or spray it with Feliway, so that it feels more alluring to her. Move it to a different place, out of the line of vision of the window so that stalker cats outside can't eyeball her. Spend time with her in the gym, perhaps using a laser pointer to encourage her to run around it. Once she gets into the habit, there may be no stopping her.

She doesn't want to wear her collar. Does she have to?

She's hooked on a branch with her leg around her head, straining to get away. Such are the dangers of the standard collar. Thank goodness for technology. Now your cat can have an injectable microchip that carries her personal ID and allows exclusive entrance through your home's cat flap. The old bell around the neck is an obvious indication that your cat is 'owned' without the use of a specialized scanner, but listen to her on this one. If it's causing her grief, get her microchipped and let her have her way.

Give her tablets?
You must be joking!

The days of the tablet-dodging moggies have been and gone. You can now give worm and flea doses using liquids that are dropped onto the skin. An antibiotic injection is available that lasts for a full two weeks, and a steroid injection can be given that persists for a month. When daily medication is unavoidable, palatable drops that are much more difficult for her to spit out than tablets are often available. If tablets are an absolute must, get some professional pill-giving lessons from the vet. Just don't let your cat see you picking up the towel before you've grabbed her.

Author biography

Peter Wedderburn is a vet in a 'companion animal' practice working only with pets. He writes a weekly column in the *Daily Telegraph* and the *Evening Irish Herald* and appears regularly as 'Pete the Vet' on Ireland's TV3. He lives in County Wicklow, Ireland, with his wife and two daughters and a menagerie of animals and birds.